Now You're a Tattoo Artist, So What's Next?

Tips to Help You Get an Artist Feature and Sponsorship

By Jarris A. H. V. Vonzombie

Book One

Now You're a Tattoo Artist, So What's Next?
Tips to Help You Get an Artist Feature and Sponsorship

Copyright © 2016 by Jarris A. H. V. Vonzombie
http://www.VONZOMBIE.com

All rights reserved. No part of this book may be reproduced or transmitted in any form or by any means without written permission from the author.

ISBN 9781674268811
Series: Book 1
2nd Edition – 12.10.2019

Printed in the USA by Inky Publications

Dedication

I dedicate my first published book with many more to come to my long-time friend, wife, and companion; ***Deanna (DeeDee) L. Vonzombie.***

Without her patience, support, dedication, love, and financial savvy as an accountant, I would not have been able to achieve so many of my dreams and goals within our life together.

This book is dedicated to my children, **Lakotah**, **Jaren**, **Jaeda**, **Shanoa**, and **Rhiannon**, as well as my friend *Hondo Hunter* for his inspirational statements, humorous personality, and the wisdom he has passed on to me over the years.

I have also included my current sponsors in this book dedication because without their endorsement and sponsorship of me as an artist, I would not have been able to create this book;

Jason Paul Drum, *Machine Builder/ Entrepreneur*
Medieval Irons Custom Tattoo Machines and Supply Co.
http://www.MedievalTattooSupply.com

Eddie Tana, Tattoo Artist/ Entrepreneur
Element Tattoo Supply Co. / OC Tattoo Studio
www.ElementTattooSupply.com

Nick Moore, Businessman/ Designer/ Ski Bum
BE Headwear Company
www.BEHeadwear.com

Table of Contents

Introduction 6

Chapter 1 **Tattooing Today** 13

Chapter 2 **Goals** 16

Chapter 3 **Style** 22

Chapter 4 **The Portfolio** 28

Chapter 5 **Artist Success** 34

Chapter 6 **Getting Featured** 43

Chapter 7 **Sponsorship** 48

Chapter 8 **Responsibilities** 56

Chapter 9 **Conclusion** 64

Introduction

I am a full-time professional artist who has been published in magazines and is currently endorsed by a few companies supplying the tattoo industry. Yes, I said 'industry,' ah, but you've never heard of me. That's okay, because there are thousands of tattoo artists around the world who are corporate-sponsored, have a large social media following, magazine features, won awards, and are completely unknown by admirers or connoisseurs of the tattoo art form. Today, what a great number of people know about the tattoo industry or the specialists within is based on what they learn watching reality television and what they read in the major tattoo magazines. I happen to be one of the many thousands of unknown artists on this great big blue planet.

I received my first tattoo during the summer of 1991, when I was 19 years old. I went to a small boardwalk studio on Venice Beach, located in Los Angeles, California, where I grew up. I remember how the tattooist looked but not his name. He was wearing a tank top, colorful board shorts, flip-flops, and had his long blondish brown hair pulled back into a ponytail. The tattooist pulled a large book with images from under a desk and with a smile, said I could pick out an image for my first tattoo. I looked through the book, which had hundreds of various designs. I later learned this book contained what was called flash art. I selected a colored bear claw within a tribal sun design. The tattooist assured me that it was a good design to go with my skin tone. I chose to have the piece placed on my left shoulder. The first punch of the needle was very surprising, but I sat through the procedure, grinning, and bearing it. That tattoo, my first tattoo, was the beginning of an 'addiction' and love for the tattoo art form. Today, my arms, neck, chest, back, and legs contain many styles of tattoo art, from American traditional, Polynesian, horror portraits to Japanese inspired tattoo art.

I consider myself a modern visual artist that specializes in creative writing, fine art, and tattoo. I have sold my paintings to various collectors around the world, but tattooing is the ultimate art form. I say this because tattoo requires focus, skill, technique, and attention to detail, plus the tattoo artist is required to capture his client's tattoo vision precisely. The artist may never get a second opportunity. There is no room for error or mistake, because we the artists, can't just start over like with a painting on cloth canvas. Tattooing is a challenge in and of itself; not every artist can tattoo! I love working with the living canvas, the human skin, because it can be delicate as rice paper due to age, or it could be tough like woven cotton canvas. The different textures and tones of human skin can also present additional challenges for an artist. Also, as an artist, a tattoo artist specifically, I have been allowed to sell my artwork almost every day instead of selling one art piece every couple of months, plus I think it's awesome to know my tattoo art may travel the world.

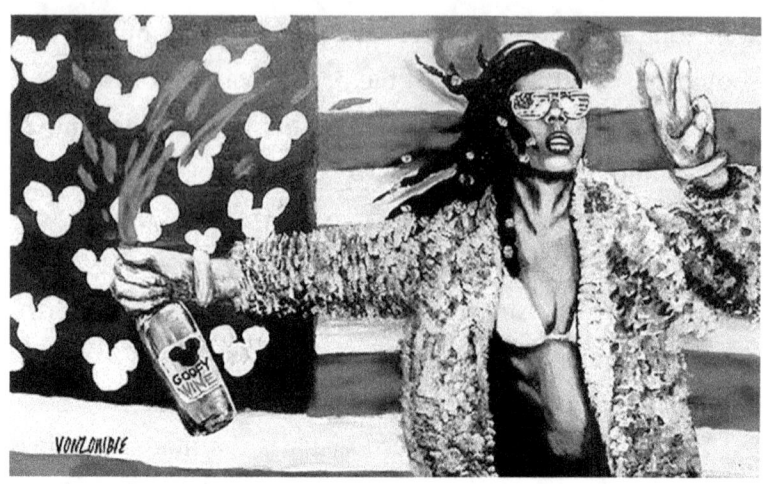
Painting by Jarris Vonzombie | Kindle book contains color photo

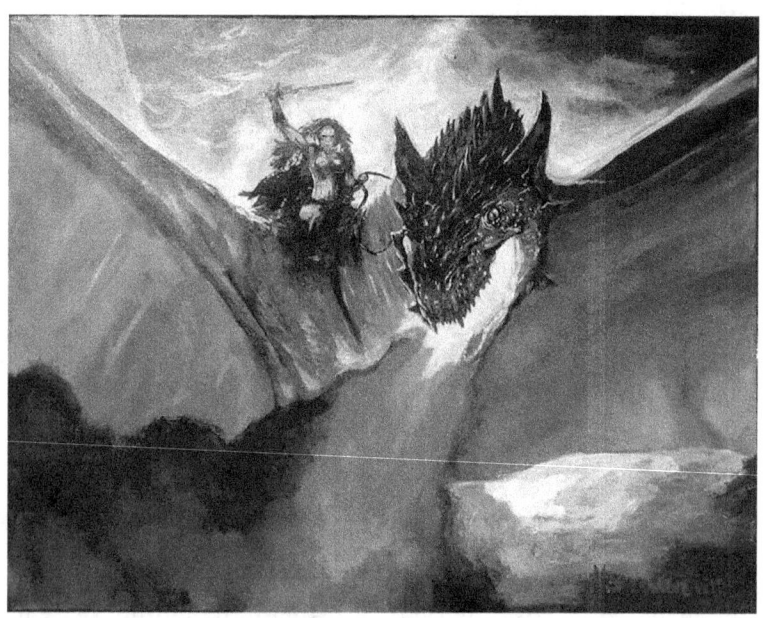
Painting by Jarris Vonzombie | Kindle book contains color photo

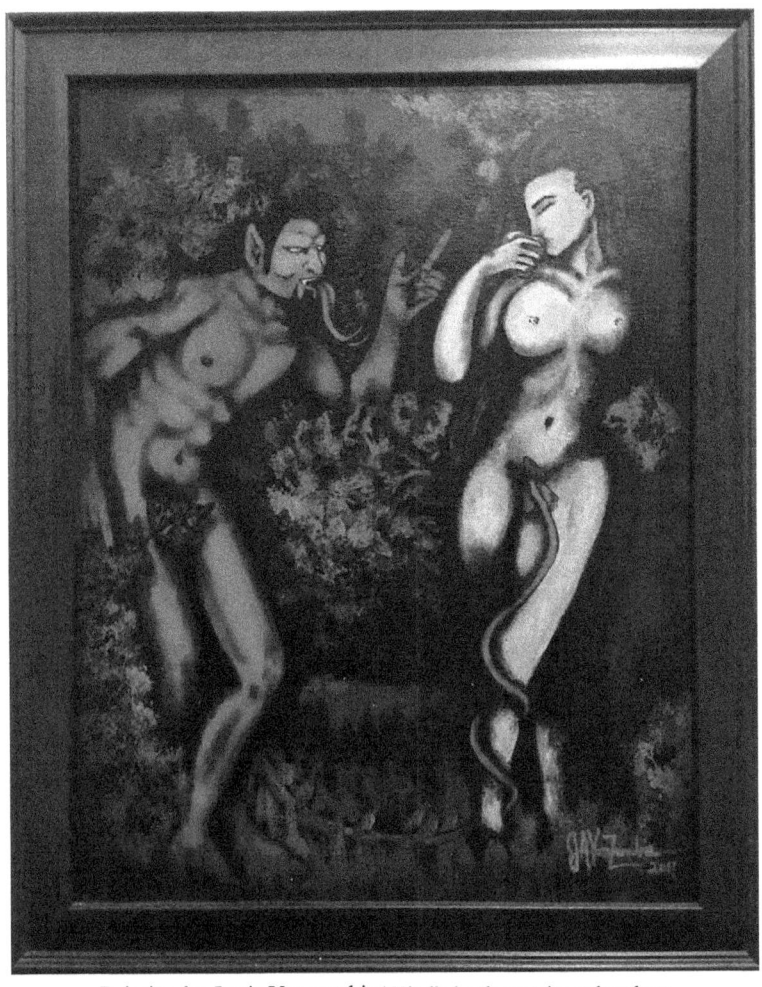

Painting by Jarris Vonzombie | Kindle book contains color photo

I have been working as an entrepreneur within and around the tattoo world since 2004, and this when I decided to open and manage my first tattoo studio. It was just me as the manager/ owner and one experienced artist until about 2007. My actual journey as an artist didn't begin until 2008 when I opened my second studio, then my third studio in 2011. Running both studios with my beautiful wife DeeDee, I was still primarily managing and learning how to tattoo in my spare time, expanding my knowledge of the tattoo industry. During my years as a studio manager, budding body piercer and "part-time" tattooist, I considered myself only a tattooist at the time because I was only re-creating flash tattoo art. In many ways, this was my apprenticeship because I learned directly from the artists in my studio on how to select the correct needles, use the machine properly, and improve my knowledge of the art form.

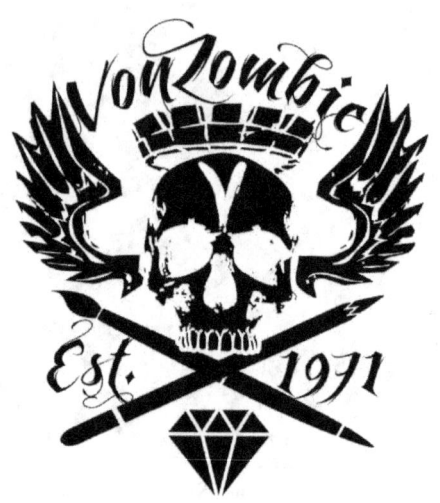

In January of 2013, after changing the name of the third studio to the family last name (for branding purposes), I officially became a full-time professional tattoo artist with an established 'returning' clientele. I learned that to be a successful artist; I had to devote 100% percent of my time to the art form. I had left my full-time government JOB after more than 20 years of service within the fields of public safety, law enforcement, and emergency management. So began my full adventure in the world of tattoo art.

Earlier that year, Jeff Ockinga, a veteran tattoo artist trained in the style of American traditional, pulled me aside one day and advised me I was doing well with the flash tattoos I had created during the short time we worked together. He had drawn up a couple of traditional tattoo machines and told me that I needed to choose one. Jeff said I had earned a machine, and he wanted to tattoo the machine on me.

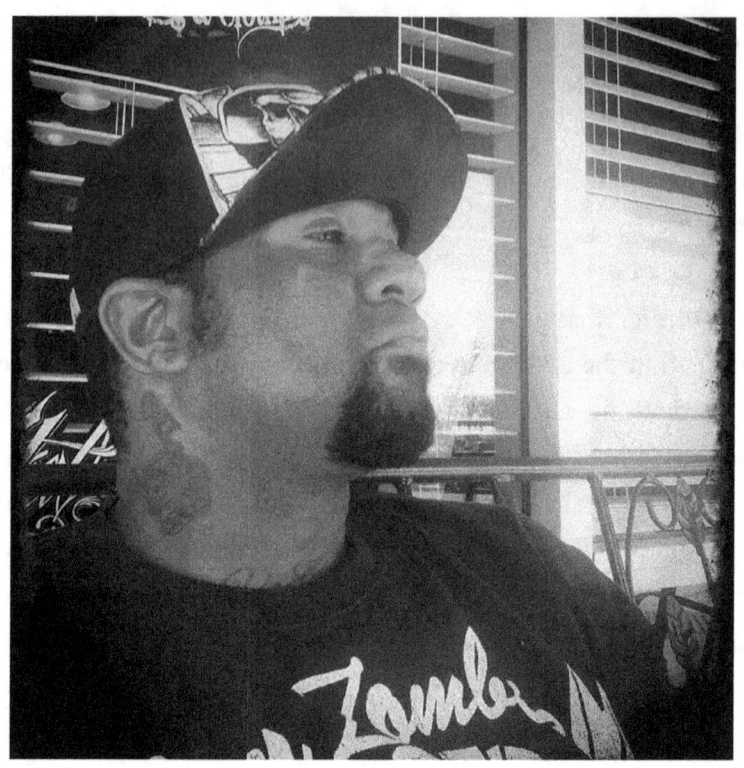

Artist Jarris Vonzombie | Kindle book contains color photo

    I was pretty damn excited to learn that Jeff had so much confidence in my abilities as a tattooist, he wanted to leave a permanent mark to show my affiliation with the industry. I had never thought about getting a tattoo machine placed on my body as a tattoo. Well, I chose to have the tattoo placed on my neck where I could show it off. Yeah, it hurt like hell, but that tattoo machine on the side of my neck was an honor and a reminder of the art form I struggled to learn and an industry I wanted to be a part of as an artist.

I created this book because I have been asked many times about how I was able to get published in magazines and sponsored only being a full-time professional artist for a short amount of time. I also thought that if I created this book, it would answer those questions and help fellow artists achieve their goals of success, notoriety, and financial growth. I am just going to tell you what I had done to get my work published and how I was able to get sponsorship from various companies supporting the tattoo world.

Chapter One
TATTOOING TODAY
So what's it all about?

The art of the tattoo has changed over the years. Though tattoo procedures are still, unfortunately, being created in someone's kitchen or dirty garage. Government oversight has increased, which improved studio/parlor operations and raised health standards in the industry with many states requiring artist licensing and bloodborne pathogens certification. If you're a veteran artist with over twenty years, you probably remember friends and family going to the guy that has a homemade tattoo "gun" and "scratches" on the side when he needs the extra cash. Though some folks still send their loved ones to that guy, the tattoo industry is fast becoming recognized as a viable art profession and career.

Today tattoo is a multi-million dollar business. The explosion of social media, reality shows, and various competitions have pulled the tattoo out of the dark and into the light, and not just any light, the spotlight! Celebrities, Musicians Athletes, Business Professionals, Politicians, and Academia have adorned their living canvases with the tattoo, many of which publicly display their ink for all to see and admire. So like a giant snowball from an avalanche, the art of tattoo and the attraction to the art form has wiped out many of the urban myths and taboo that having a tattoo once held. This form of art is no longer solely for the soldier, sailor, ex-con, criminal, gang member or biker. Tattoo studios and parlors are located on main boulevards, in hotels, and shopping malls.

The tattoo is now mainstream, and like most anything that forces the general public to swallow it whole, involving big business, whether we as artists like it or not. However, this is not a bad thing for those of us who want to prosper in an 'industry' that is currently being flooded by many very talented tattooists and artists. Meaning real competition between artists and 'studios' to grow clientele, receive high earnings and be recognized for one's talents and abilities. Tattoo related supply companies and clothing brands have popped up over the last decade due to demand, and with demand comes competition for them as well. Yep, the art of tattoo has come a long way, and so has the terminology. The mechanical instrument used to create tattoo art upon the human flesh for medical marking, adornment, and beautification is no-longer referred to as a "gun", but as a "machine," this is as important as those persons working within the tattoo industry recognizing that they are highly paid and trained professionals providing a service.

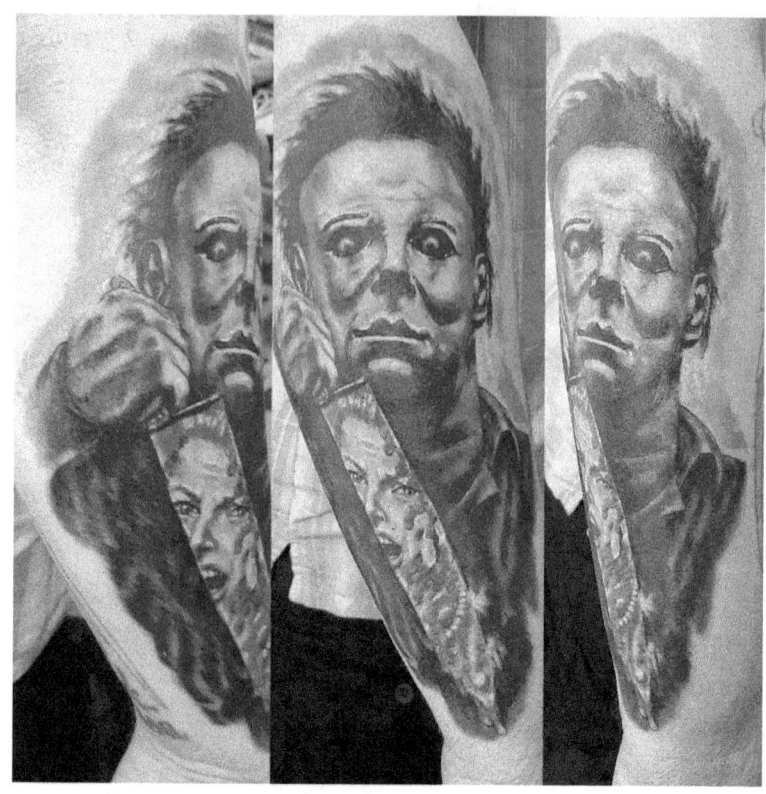

Tattoo Art by Jarris Vonzombie | Kindle book contains color photo

So long, we say to the days of the starving artist, who had hoped to sell only one painting in their lifetime. As a tattoo artist, you sell your style and technique of fine art almost every day, whether it be script, flash or custom. You are an artist, creating fine art on a very difficult and ever-changing canvas of different colors, tones, shades, thickness, fresh or aged with personality. This means you have to convince your client, a human being, aka the living canvas, that you are the most qualified to create fine art upon their precious flesh.

Chapter Two
GOALS
What's the Strategy?

So, I ask you the reader and artist these simple questions. Do you have a business plan as an independent artist? What do you want to achieve as an artist? Do you want to leave a legacy? Keep in mind, unlike fine art on a fabric canvas, your tattoo art only lasts as long as the living canvas wearing it. You, the artist, have to properly document your living canvas art masterpieces in the digital form through photograph and video. Share your talents with the world by getting your tattoo work published in magazines or books, work conventions, enter your living canvases in tattoo competitions, and utilizing social media as well as a professionally built website as your portfolio.

So let's say you have done all of those tasks mentioned above, what's next? Well, the world of endorsement and company sponsorship is knocking at your door. The almost rock star and celebrity status of many tattoo artists call for companies to build collectives and teams of top artists to promote and sell their products to customers, as well as to the up and coming. Tips on how you can become a featured and sponsored artist will be explained later in this book. First, let's talk about how to set goals as it relates to you getting a magazine feature and obtaining endorsements.

Let's jump back to 2013 when I became recognized by my peers as a professional tattoo artist. That was the year of enlightenment for me, and I had to think about where I wanted to go with this newfound feeling of recognition. I already understood the aspect of running a successful tattoo studio and business, but now I had to learn how to run myself so I could be a successful tattoo artist, well let's say, artist. The reason why I am eliminating tattoo from the artist title is that being an artist is the most important no matter the genre, and this book could help various other artists get the recognition they feel they deserve, so they too can leave a legacy.

What I decided to do was set goals for myself. The best way to set goals is to write them down in a notebook or on a sheet of paper that you can pin to a corkboard. Writing them down lets the universe know you are ready to move forward, making them more tangible, and will be there visually to remind you what still needs to be accomplished. I created my goals list by writing down and thinking about what I wanted to accomplish as an artist and businessman. What I drafted is as follows, keep in mind this applied to what was happening in my world at the time.

Change of Business Related Responsibilities

I wanted to be treated as an artist in my studio, not as an owner or manager. So I had to have a studio manager work with my wife in the handling of the daily studio operation.

Learn How to Create a Particular Style of Tattoo

Now that I had changed my areas of responsibility. I wanted to figure out what style of tattoo art would I most excel within. I needed to learn what type of tattoo I was good at creating. Yep, this took a few months to figure out, but it wasn't that challenging because I loved the look of realism and hyper-realism tattoo art.

I set out on a treasure hunt by tracking down and purchasing instructional videos and books produced by top world-renowned realism tattoo artists who specialized in portraits, wildlife, figurative and still life art. I even purchased memberships to tattoo techniques and education websites hosted by these top artists. I studied every technique given to me and with that, I tried every type of machine that I thought would help me improve upon the techniques I was learning. So with that, I also suggest finding an artist that you most admire with regards to their style of tattoo art and techniques. For me, I chose about three realism artists that I wanted my tattoos to resemble. At some point, you gain your technique within your chosen style of tattoo art. Find a mentor or an artist to follow that uses a technique to create the style of tattoo you want to learn.

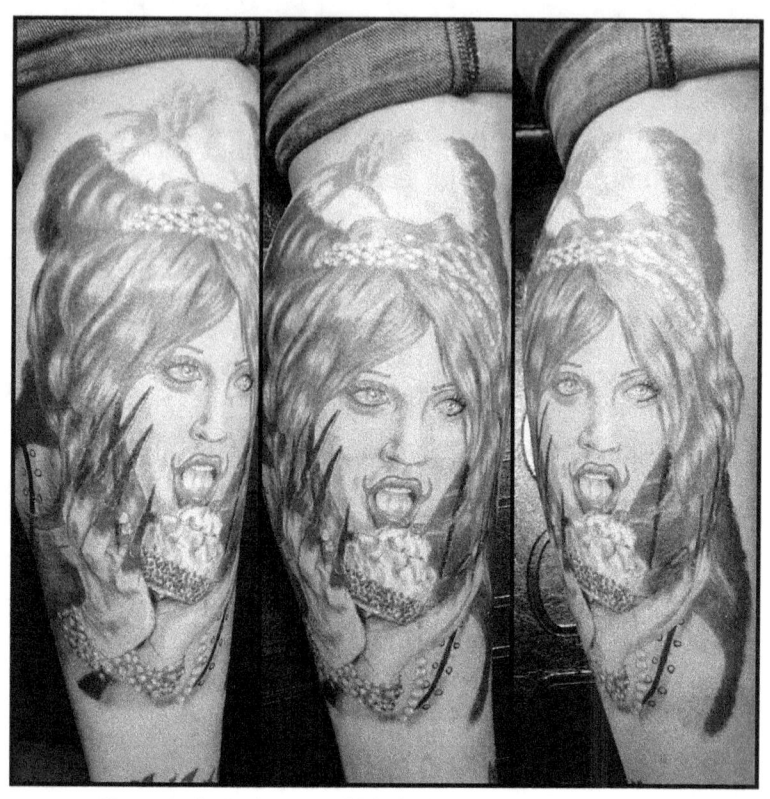

Tattoo Art by Jarris Vonzombie | Kindle book contains color photo

Learn to Take Quality Portfolio Photographs

So now, it is on to, how do I capture my tattoo art in the form of a photograph? I noticed the top artists had maybe only 20 to 30 or so 8"x10" high-quality tattoo art photos in their portfolios. I was honestly used to seeing low-quality tattoo photos as a 4"x6" picture in a portfolio of 100 or so photos. I remember in one of my instructional videos, it was stated that a well-done tattoo should be able to be enlarged to an 8"x10" print and that having a portfolio of 4"x6" pictures was deceptive and the client cannot see the true quality of the artist's work. The artist who has faith in his tattoo artwork, should create large prints of their artwork for their portfolio and limit the number of prints to 20 pictures. The photograph is integral to the continuity of the artist's portfolio; therefore, I needed to learn how to take the best pictures I possibly could.

Learn How to Properly Submit Artwork to Publications.

So with the goals mentioned above, I added a couple more goals related to where I wanted this new-found knowledge to take me. I wanted to get my tattoo artwork in magazines. For years I have been reading tattoo magazines, studying the art, who's hot, and what's new. I currently have tattoo magazines dating back to the late '90s. So how do I get my tattoo artwork published and eventually become a featured artist? I needed to contact and 'speak' to publishers and ask how to get published in their magazines or on their websites.

Learn About Endorsements, Co-Branding and Being a Brand Representative.

Contact and 'speak' to branding managers or company owners about becoming an endorsed artist. I figured that after I was able to gain a few published tattoos, articles, and features, I could move onto the final goal. I wanted to not only to become a published artist but to become an endorsed/ sponsored artist.

Wow, I know, but you have to think big, and this is just the first set of goals because once you reach these goals, you have to set new goals to further excel your career as a recognized and endorsed professional artist. We will talk about more about that in another book. For now, let's get you an endorsement deal. Just like in the saying, "…with great power comes a greater responsibility!" endorsements can be seen in a similar light, "…with great endorsements comes even more responsibility!"

Well, I felt that if I obtained an endorsement from a company or two within the tattoo industry, I would be gaining additional recognition from my peers, as well as having some form of professional status to my clientele. Probably the most difficult of all the goals.

I set a time frame to complete my goals. I reasonably believed that I could achieve all of my goals within two years. My first year was establishing my style, perfecting my technique while further establishing myself and my name as a brand. I researched what companies looked for, when they sponsored artists and athletes, as well figured out what editors of magazines want to publish. My second year was all about getting published, and my third-year focus was on taking all that I had accomplished and presenting it to companies to gain an endorsement or artist sponsorship.

Chapter Three
STYLE
Genre and Niche

So what's your style, what genre do you prefer and do you have a niche that separates you from other tattoo artists in your area? A question I had asked myself. I learned that artists might be able to create all forms of tattoo work, but there is a particular style or two in which they excel. I excelled at realism in the form of portraiture, wildlife, sealife, figurative and still life. For some reason, the way I see the world as a tattoo artist is that I love earth tones and natural colors. Realism allowed me to use a lot of colors. So from this self-discovery, I established that my style is realism. Then I later learned that I love to create fantasy and horror-based genre pieces, especially when inspired by movie monster characters or themes.

Finding what you are great at creating is your next step to accomplishing your goals. There are niche markets in the tattoo industry. For example, if you want American traditional, you don't go to a realism artist, it's like going to a brain specialist for symptoms related to cardiology. Yes, the brain specialist is a doctor and could probably diagnose cardiology problems, but you will most likely get more accurate results from a trained cardiologist. So are you a jack of all styles, but a master of none? Well, this is what you want to avoid. Yes, Tattoo artists should be well-rounded. However, the goal of this book is to help you stand apart from your local competition and get noticed. Your focus from this point forward should be to establish yourself to become well known and recognized for what you, as a tattoo artist, are great at creating.

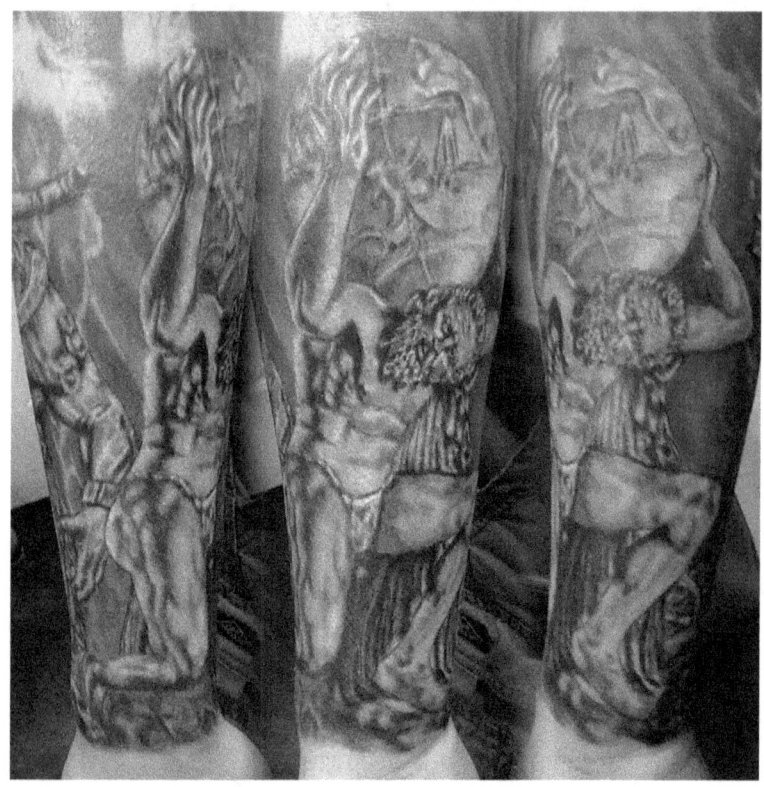

Tattoo Art by Jarris Vonzombie | Kindle book contains color photo

There are many different paths you can take to find your style that makes your style unique and sought after. Just like anything we seek to do in the world as creative entrepreneurial humans, we learn that one-size does not fit all! The quickest route to being recognized, no matter what

you do for a living, is to figure out your art style by doing the following;
1. Find a niche
2. Focus on that niche; and
3. Create a great portfolio within that niche.

So I am sure you're asking, "How do I find my niche and my style?" My answer is, "The best niche and style to focus on is the one that you feel the most passionate about!" Like I recently explained, my passion is realism tattoo art. Your passion could be Traditional Japanese, Neo-Traditional, Trash Polka or even Dotwork, but you will never know until trying each style and figure out which one makes your heart race.

The assumption is you are currently a tattoo artist, and you love what you're doing. Meaning, you'll also do your best work when you are creating an art piece related to the style and genre in which you are most interested, basically your niche in an ever-growing and changing market. The power of the niche is determined by the adage "big fish in a little pond" ideology. It is more likely that you can become well known in the tattoo industry when you focus in one small area.

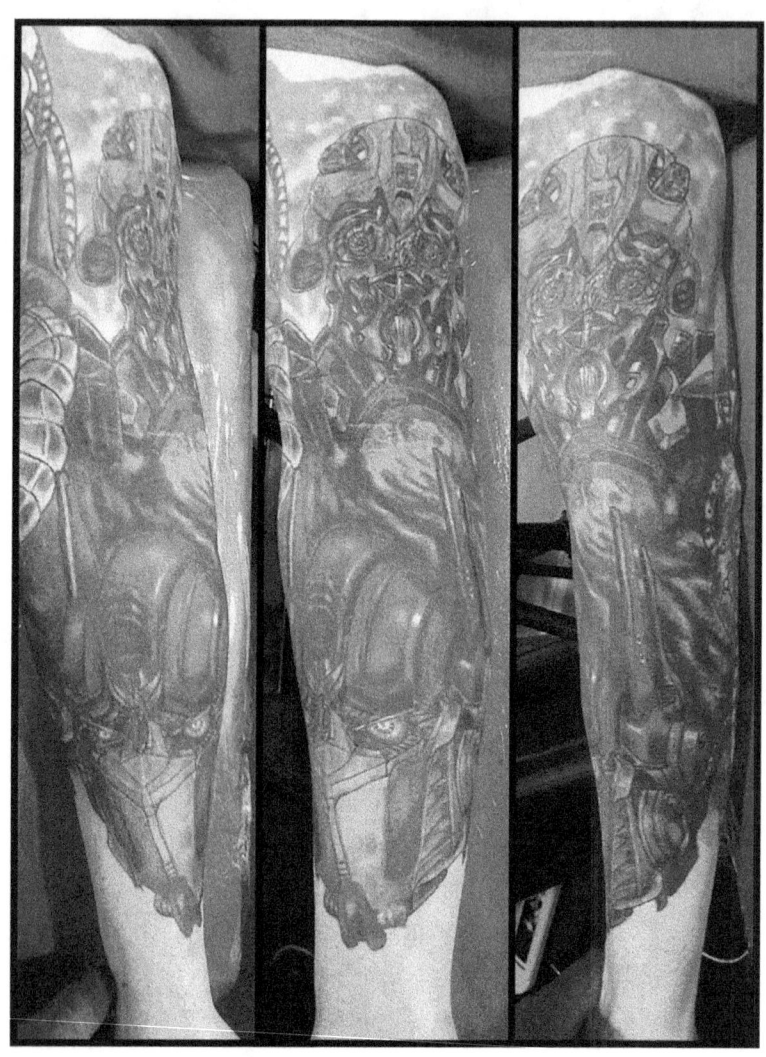

Tattoo Art by Jarris Vonzombie | Kindle book contains color photo

You can't be all things to all clients! I have personally never heard anyone say, "There's John Smith, he is a tattoo artist, and he is well known for doing every style of tattoo art imaginable!" I know of tattoo artists who create tattoos in many different styles, genres, and subject matters; they try to be all things to every client. They ultimately get lost in the shuffle, because they have become a little fish in a huge pond. It's okay not to have an actual niche, but if you want to become known for your style, you have to focus in one area. Listed below are a few different areas in which you can find your niche.

Becoming Known for Your Style and Genre
Some artists have an unmistakable style, you don't have to see their name on the work to know they did it. Examples would be Salvador Dali and Picasso. However, whatever you do, don't become known as the guy who knocks off other tattoo artists! Be original in your tattoo art designs. Clients like to show their artists pictures from the internet of tattoos they want or like. Remember they are just examples. Don't just copy that tattoo from the picture, create a similar design using your style and vision. The majority of clients will understand this, and this is why nowadays, I don't like creating tattoos from flash and prefer realism. If you have a distinctive style, you will eventually become known for it. This ideology can apply to almost any business model i.e., Author, Musician, Fine Artist, Sculptor, etc.

There are authors known for writing novels that can unsettle our nerves and scare us with things that go bump in the night! Many focused their creative writing style on writing horror, suspense and science fiction stories.

Here are some suggestions to help you find your style and niche;
1. What do I love doing most?
2. (Think of tattoo art that makes your brows raise and your eyes widen.)
3. What style makes me happiest?
4. (Think design aspects)
5. What do I feel passionate about?
6. (Think styles, techniques, and genres)
7. Reflect on something you've created in the past:
8. Why was it so easy for me?
9. Was it the client, the style, the project, the genre, or something else?

Then ask yourself this final question:

Where do I WANT to focus my time and efforts?

Be kind to yourself and give yourself a bit of time to determine your direction. Often, the answers are right there, and we don't realize it to will sit back and think about it. There is a reason why finding your style and niche is so powerful. When you focus your attention on one area, staying aware of all that is around you, and you consistently work on that one area, improving that one technique and style, you will get better, then perfection soon follows. Eventually, you will become the go-to person for that particular style within a certain genre related to that niche.

Chapter Four
THE PORTFOLIO
Photography and Video Diaries

Learning to take a great portfolio picture with proper lighting and angle is like making a good first impression when meeting someone. Your photo will determine whether that client hires you for their tattoo project, or a publisher chooses your tattoo to feature in their magazine. There are many books and website articles out there about basic smartphone cameras and or digital camera operations. I apologize for not having any recommendations, but they are not hard to find. Use a keyword search or term like How to properly photograph a tattoo.

When taking a picture of your portfolio, there are many factors to consider. However, here is what I do to create my physical and digital portfolio. My standard approach for capturing tattooing images by using the camera attached to my smartphone with the grid activated. If you don't have a smartphone, then use a digital camera that uses over 10 megapixels. Most magazines will accept digital photos, as long as they do not have photo filters or modifications. A modified photo is a tattoo picture that was manipulated through a program to be more than what it is. Doing this is deceptive and a big No-No! I suggest also creating a tattoo video diary related to the process of creating the tattooed piece. Use a video to capture the before, stencil application, the outline, the halfway point and the conclusion.

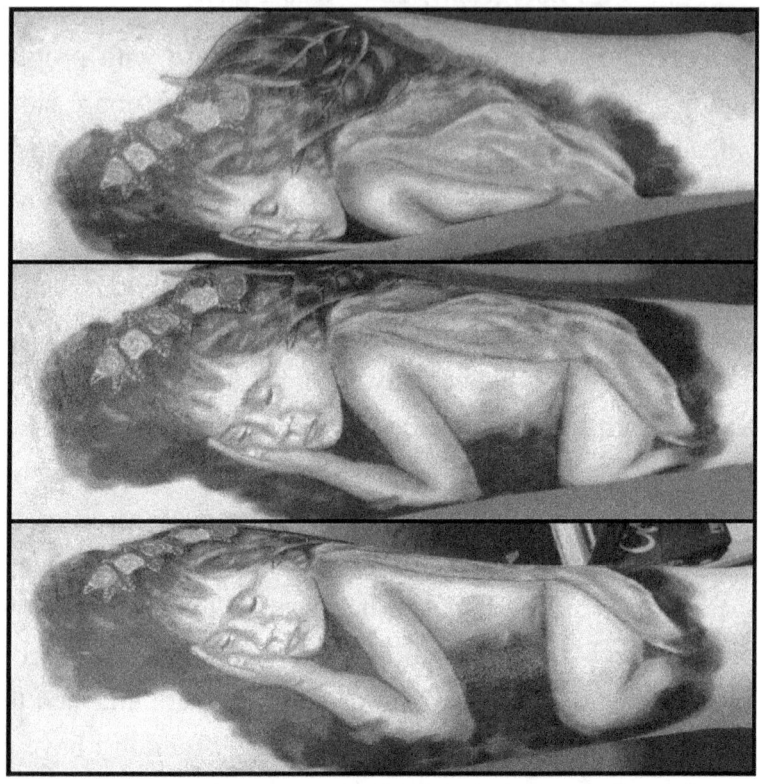

Tattoo Art by Jarris Vonzombie | Kindle book contains color photo

Photos tell a great story, but a video of your tattoo art under proper lighting conditions tell a much better story about the quality of your work. I normally take about 2 to 5 pictures of every tattoo before choosing the right one to post to my digital portfolio. When I photograph the fresh tattoo, I try to get slightly different vantage points, angles, and distances. Keep in mind the photo of the tattoo should be clear and properly lit because a physical portfolio picture should be at least 8"x10" in size. Most importantly, don't forget to watermark your photo with your name and/ or logo before posting to any website or social media account.

Photographing and Video Recording a Fresh Tattoo

When you have completed the tattoo procedure, allow your client to get up and stretch their legs, this gets the blood flowing and allows them to relax. The body regains circulation in the tattooed area and allows the details from the new pigment to be more visible. Tattoos generally "weep" plasma for about 20 minutes to 3 hours after a tattoo is complete. So there are some things I can suggest you do to optimize your photos. When I complete a tattoo, I like to soak a paper towel with witch hazel and place it on the tattooed area to cool the skin, lessen the swelling around the tattooed area, and reduce the redness. The plasma and sometimes exposed blood that surfaces during weeping potentially makes the tattoo artwork appear muddy and alter the color of the pigment in a photo or video. After the client has had the opportunity to relax post-tattoo, glove up and gently wipe off the plasma with a damp paper towel. You can use a dry paper towel to blot away glare. Change to fresh gloves to handle your camera or cell phone with one hand, and blotting away glare with the freehand if necessary. Avoid cross-contamination while taking your photos.

Photographing and Video Recording a Healed Tattoo

I love taking photos of and video recordings of my client's healed tattoos, allowing me to scrutinize my work, as well as allowing future clients to see how a particular tattoo artwork has healed. So the first train of thought is to shave the healed tattoo area. It is not advisable to photograph or video a tattoo covered in hair; it will dramatically take away from the tattoo. Before taking any pics or videos, use some lotion on that tattoo. Allow the lotion to soak in for a few minutes, and if necessary, blot it down to remove excess lotion and glare.

The following are what I try to keep in mind when photographing my tattoo artwork;

1. Avoid using a flash. Camera flash produces glare; it can also mute certain pigment tones and may cause the tattoo to look inflamed.

2. Be aware of your surroundings. What's in your background? Avoid objects in the background that will make you look unprofessional, like carpet. Utilize a plain single color painted wall that has a satin finish; white tends to reflect light onto the tattoo altering contrast, and using black for a background is optimal for the best picture.

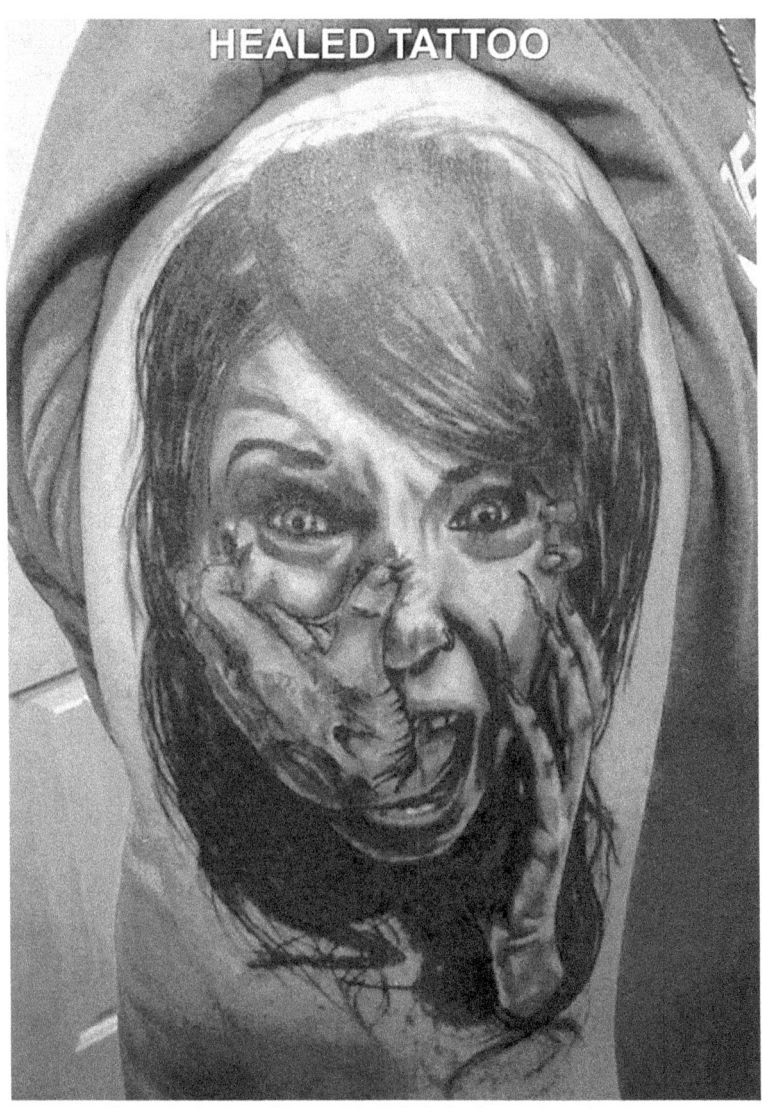

Tattoo Art by Jarris Vonzombie | Kindle book contains color photo

3. Think about your lighting. Certain bulbs can change the coloring within your tattoo. Use natural, but shaded outdoor sunlight, or when indoors use white light. I would say avoid soft white bulbs or soft white fluorescent lighting. Position your client in a way shadows are not being cast down onto the tattoo, or position your lighting in a way to eliminate shadows.

There is no need to be right on top of the tattoo, but let's not make it a distance shot either. If you need help taking a photo, then get help. Editing photos or videos that were taken with your smartphone or device is extremely simple nowadays, locate the best app, read reviews, then proceed to get your portfolio picture ready to be posted to your social media site or website. Don't forget to crop the client's tattoo, eliminating any unwanted background noise. I like to crop my photos into a square. Remember, do not use photo filters with your portfolio tattoo pictures, but do remember to watermark your photos with your name or logo so that when your artwork is on a worldwide web social platform, anyone seeing the picture will know how to find you. Yes, there is an app for watermarking photos and videos too. One thing I learned is that you have to have a set of photos of your work without watermarks for submission to magazines, and the quality of your photos should be about 300 dpi and no smaller than 800 x 800 pixels.

Chapter Five
ARTIST SUCCESS
Branding and Networking

Let's talk about personal branding. Probably one of the most important, but overlooked and disregarded subject matters related to business that artists fail to realize the importance. Personal blogs and social media sites like Facebook, Twitter and Instagram have enabled us to become known. We can connect in almost real-time immediately and directly with clients, colleagues, family, and friends. Technology has allowed us to build relationships with people all over the world. Even language is no longer a barrier with the advent of translator apps. We are no longer bound to make our first impressions in person; we can now establish our brand virtually and globally.

Who you are and how you come across are important to being successful at anything you do. Individually, our personal brand is in the spotlight every day. We are online sharing our moments and memories for everyone to see. So the question I have for you is, are you as an artist putting your best foot forward? If not, then maybe it's time for you to consider personal and professional branding. Well, if you don't brand yourself, then you allow someone else to create your personal and professional brand for you. The result of such a transaction will not be in your favor. Let me put it to you this way, branding yourself keeps you current as an artist. As you will learn later in this book, branding yourself will open doors for you and create a lasting impression on potential and existing clients, as well as companies you wish to be endorsed by and magazines in which you wish to be published or featured. The development of your brand will allow you to have control over the initial perception people have of you as a professional, an entrepreneur, a business person, and, most importantly, an artist.

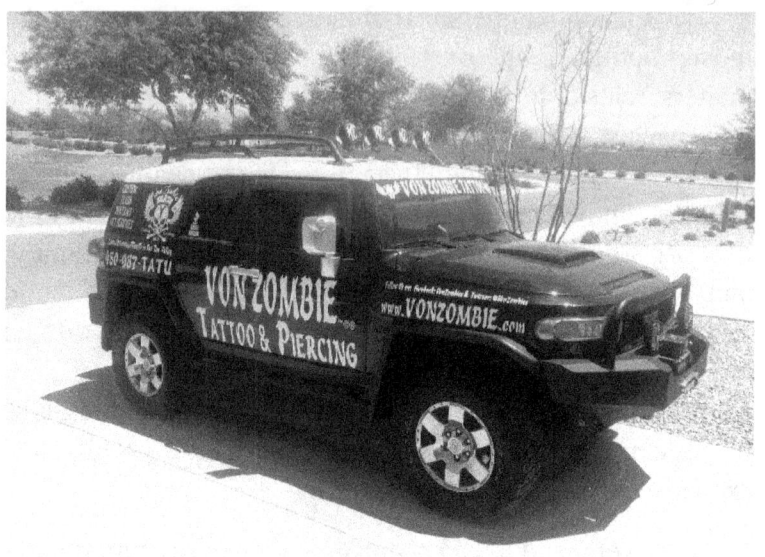

Photo Courtesy of Vonzombie Studio | Kindle book contains color photo

So what is it that you want to be known for? Personal branding is how we define ourselves, personally, and professionally. These days, branding your tattoo studio or parlor isn't enough because the world wants to hear what YOU have to say and what YOU have to offer. All I can say is that if you are not building your own personal and professional brand, your tattoo business will suffer. You are officially known as a tattoo artist and for your business to be successful, you must become an expert in your field, claim a website under your domain name (i.e., YourFullNameTattoo.com or YourFullNameArt.com or just YourFullName.com), connect with social media, and build relationships with your clientele, which is just one half of your total audience.

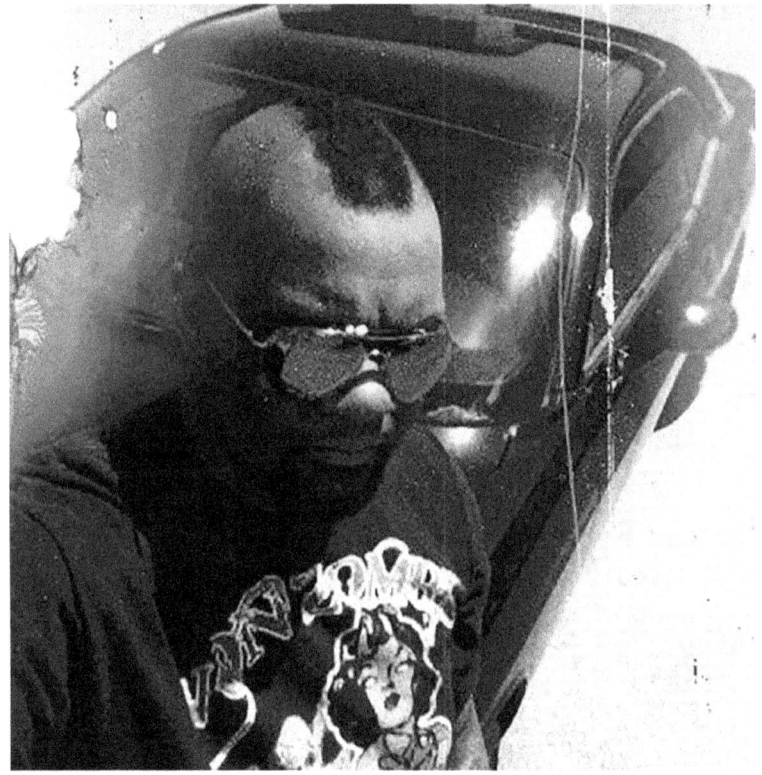

Artist Jarris Vonzombie | Kindle book contains color photo

So with the aforementioned in mind, here are some suggestions I have related to branding yourself;

1. Become an expert on something that relates to your services, tattoo style, and business. Artists looking to attract new clients and build their businesses should focus on becoming an expert in their field. For example, you're the owner/ artist of a tattoo studio; it's probably not wise to brand yourself as a nutrition and weight loss expert.

2. Establish a website or blog under your full name. Publications, Sponsors, and Your customers all use search engines to research you, connect with you and potentially either do business with you or interview you. This is the importance of why you need to purchase your full name as a domain name (yourfullname.com). If you are working another artist's studio and not your own, develop either a static website or a blog under your domain name, you will own the first result for your name in search engines. If you own your studio, this should be a separate site than your company's website. After purchasing your domain name, add your picture, a bio, your e-mail address, and links to the rest of your online social media presence.

3. When you're interviewed by a publication or blog, you will always be able to promote your studio through your byline, which will help build both your personal and professional brand.

4. Generate brand awareness through networking. You, as an artist, should be connecting with other entrepreneurial-minded artists in our tattoo industry, using social networks, giving positive comments on their portfolio-art pics, and tattoo video diaries, or blogs. Networking is one of the best ways to become known in the tattoo industry. Forming a positive, supportive, and honest relationship with your peers and audience will build your business, as well as the personal and professional brand for long-term success. I have learned there are four rules of networking that you should keep in mind;

a. Mutualism: You have to create win-win relationships in business, making sure that you don't benefit more than the other party.

b. Giving: Help someone out before asking for anything in return. This makes people want to support you.

c. Targeting: You want to be very specific with the types of people you network with, so to save time, and to attract the right people to your brand.

d. Reconnecting: Never lose touch; that way networking contacts remember you when new opportunities surface.

I am going to give you something else to remember and will help you along your journey. There are three Cs of branding;

1. Clarity
2. Consistency
3. Constancy.

Be clear about who you are and who you are not. Don't sugar-coat your qualifications or your abilities as an artist. Express your brand across all communications mediums, use social media. Determine where you want to fit in within the art community and tattoo industry; Style, Genre, and Niche area of expertise. Then remain visible to your target audience, stay in the spotlight. Absorb constructive criticism, which means get feedback from those who know you best- family, friends and fellow artists. The true measure of your personal and professional brand is the reputation others hold of you in their hearts and minds. So pay attention to how you are introduced to others and inquire about what your top brand attributes and core strengths are as a person, a business person, and an artist. If they, your friends, family and fellow artists can easily tell you, then you've succeeded in branding you as both the person, professional, and artist.

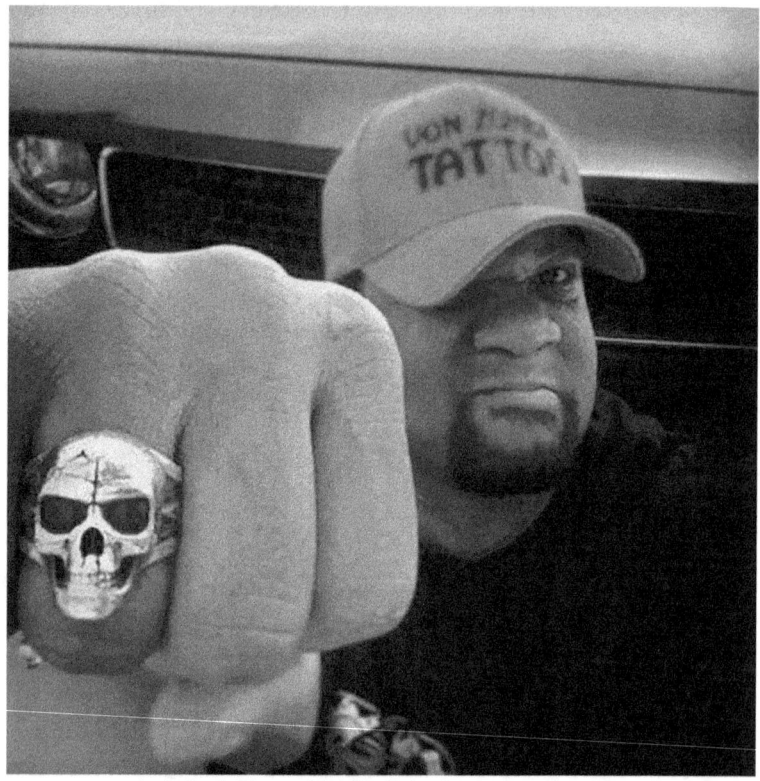

Artist Jarris Vonzombie | Kindle book contains color photo

There are other ways of branding yourself, and these ways can and should be considered in your professional artist's future. We work in a creative field, so you may want to consider using the services of a manager, an agent or a publicist depending on your level of notoriety as an artist. These individuals will help you find work and negotiate pay and work conditions. Yes, I know, many of you will say, "It's just not the way it's done as a tattooist.". However, I will tell you this, no matter your reason for wanting to become a full-time professional artist, times are changing rapidly within the tattoo industry. It is an industry currently being saturated with exceptional artists from all over the world. It is becoming very competitive, and your tattoo art is being examined, scrutinized and compared to, as well as against other artists, which is why I decided to mention those three professions because any one of those three professions will make you and your work stand out among the millions of artist — ultimately gaining you more clients. We as artists want our art sought after, and we all want our appointment booked up months in advance and/ or to be commissioned out for an entire year in advance.

Now let's talk briefly about the manager, agent, and publicist. I am going to start with the publicist because I would say this person is our starting point before we even think about obtaining an agent or manager to represent our interests.

1. A publicist helps manage our relationship with the media: i.e., magazines, blogs, etc. They arrange interviews with a journalist, prepare press announcements, deal with social media and overall help you, the artist, gain publicity. They also advise you on how to avoid unwanted publicity. Publicists tend to be associated with large firms and their rate is typically a flat fee rather than a percentage of your income. Publicists may also work on retainer, like an attorney. The publicist is your marketing

guru. They are selling you, your art, and your brand to the public, so that you can increase your clientele base.

2. The agent often has hundreds of clients. They are responsible for finding the artist's work or projects and negotiates the terms of your employment contracts. This is not common among tattoo artists unless they happen to be authors, musicians, models or actors too.

3. A manager is the combination of an agent and a publicist. They are like daddy or momma to your career because they provide guidance and career advice which may also include financial and legal advice, Managers can be more personable then agents in the fact they generally have only a few clients and spend quality time with each. The far-ranging duties of the manager include advice on what jobs to take, marketing assistance, and organization of advertising as well as publicity direction. The manager will also advise on how to better develop your talents and how to manage your income as an artist.

Now that I have covered some additional need to know information. You should be aware many in the tattoo industry frown upon this level of commitment and marketing. So I will tell you this, who cares what they think! Some artists simply cannot manage their money or their career properly. Many feel that your art alone should do all the speaking. Well, that may have been fine twenty or more years ago, but again} with the explosion of interest in the world of tattoo, nowadays, you can't just rely solely on your art to get you noticed. To get to the ocean from the pond, you have to consider at some point during your career using the expertise of professionals who have dedicated their lives to the promotion, publicity, and branding of others with specific talents sought after by the general public and companies.

Chapter Six
GETTING FEATURED
Magazines, Newspapers, and Blogs

I am sure your next question is, "How do I write an Artist Bio or Statement?" Writing a Bio can be disconcerting for most people. It can be very difficult to describe yourself on a personal level, as well as on a professional one. Take a look at bios created by other artists. Ask your family and friends how they would describe you both personally and professionally. Try to give the reader of your bio and artist statement a small glimpse into your life, about your art, and what it means to be a tattoo artist or just an artist. Don't forget to review the type and style of artwork that is being most featured, as well as the professional artist headshots, are being used. Often a magazine depending on your "status" or where you're located will do a photoshoot with you if you are a key feature of their magazine.

Getting published and getting featured is about self-promotion. If you don't promote yourself, who will? Some would agree that self-promotion sounds like a dirty word. Your livelihood as an artist depends on marketing, yet they seem to avoid and resist it. However, if you look at the successful artists who have found success, without the backing of big money, you'll find that self-promotion was a necessary piece to their success puzzle. Survival means gaining new clients and artistic opportunities, which require self-promotion. None truly cares about your success, but you. Today's internet and social media-driven world, we can be anything, sell anything and meet anyone by merely powering on our computers, allowing us as artists to attract fans and followers from all over the world.

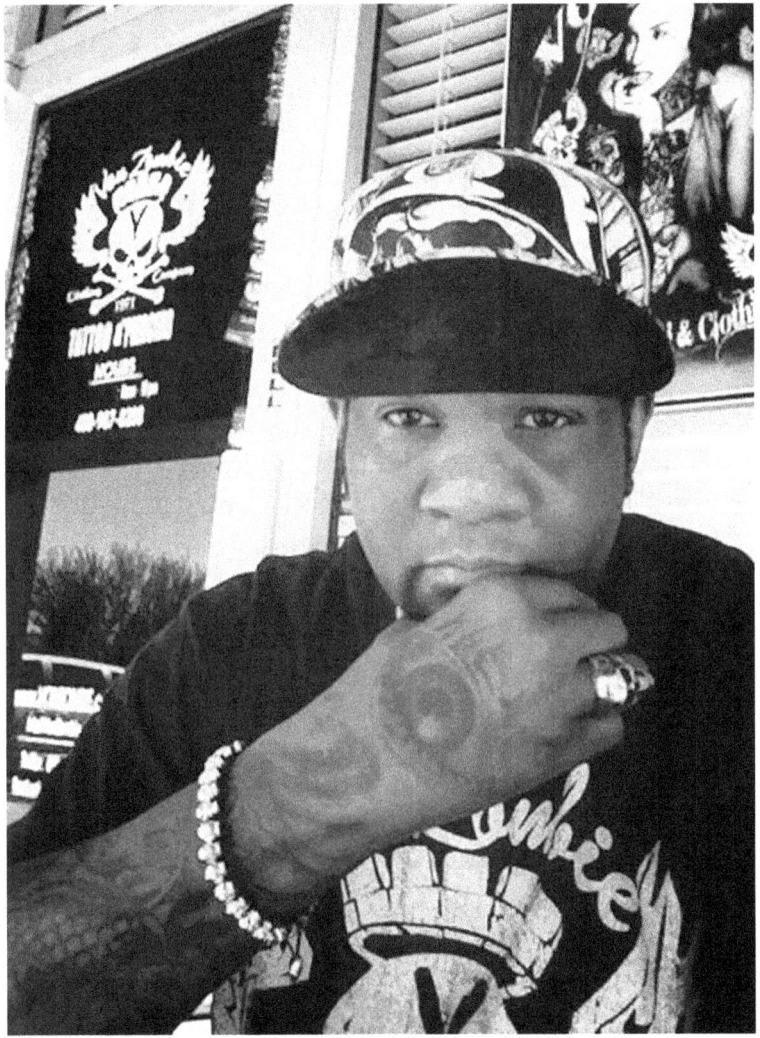

Artist Jarris Vonzombie | Kindle book contains color photo

Getting published in your favorite tattoo or lifestyle magazine can be a fairly simple process most of the time. It all starts with having impressive artwork, a unique style, creating a specific, popular, or new genre, as well as having a prepared portfolio hosted on your website or social media account. Once you have contacted a magazine editor and submitted your high quality, unaltered, non-watermarked photos with a short bio, they will often contact you via email, letting you know the issue and page(s) within which you will be featured. Editors will research you, so it is important that when you submit your work, you provide them with a link to your social media accounts and website. A feature may only be a single picture of a tattoo you created, a single page with pictures and a bio, or a full five-page spread. All of which are important for an up and coming artist.

When an issue comes out featuring you and your artwork, or even just your artwork, get that issue and document in a notepad or on your website, the issue number, and the page(s) of your feature. Then share your feature success via your favorite social media outlet. Let's say you have been rejected. Well, don't take it personally and definitely do not start hating on the publication. Just contact the editor and find out what you can do better so you can get a feature on your next submission. Sometimes a rejection is due to the quality of your submitted images, or it is as simple as your artwork doesn't fit the layout of their upcoming issue, but it could also be your skill level is not up to current industry standards.

Be in the know, and join their mailing list, because there are many times a publication is seeking fresh new artists and styles for a new issue and they will send out an email requesting submissions. You also do not want to overlook the fact that magazines with social media sites will post short articles about you the artist on their website, within their blogs, and share your artwork digitally. Snapshot, that online feature and save it, documenting the date, the writer, and the magazine. This form of publication is as important to have on your resume, as having a physical publication on your bookshelf.

Exposure = Popularity = Interest = Fans = Sales = Success

So let's say you think you're not the best artist in comparison to the top named artists in the world, but people have told you that your artwork is really good. Let me tell you a hard to swallow truth about business and art. Often the most successful people are not necessarily the most talented; however, they are the best marketed. Perception is everything. So if you get yourself and your work seen by the world and there are magazines and various other publications positively showcasing you, your brand and your work, then you are going to be perceived as a successful, talented artist, whom in time will gain a following based on how you are marketed.

There are going to be times you want a little more press and little more advertising as an artist. You can submit yourself to a publication that offers free press, or you can pay for a single page advertisement in many of the magazines featuring your artwork. These can be created in the form of a feature. Having an authority, like a newspaper or magazine or blog, write about what you're doing will give you exposure and credibility. The more credibility and exposure you receive, whether free or paid for, the more people will know about you and will trust in what you do because someone spent the time to either print your work, publish your press release, or specifically write a feature about you. The key is not to just *sell* the story of you and your art, but to *tell* the story of you and your artwork. What I am referring to is what you the artist wants to send out "newsworthy" releases, not advertisements. It often appears, just like with sponsorship, once you are published in one publication, you will most likely be featured in another publication. Getting published and featured is the start of creating your legacy as an artist, and being a press-friendly artist will lead you in the right direction.

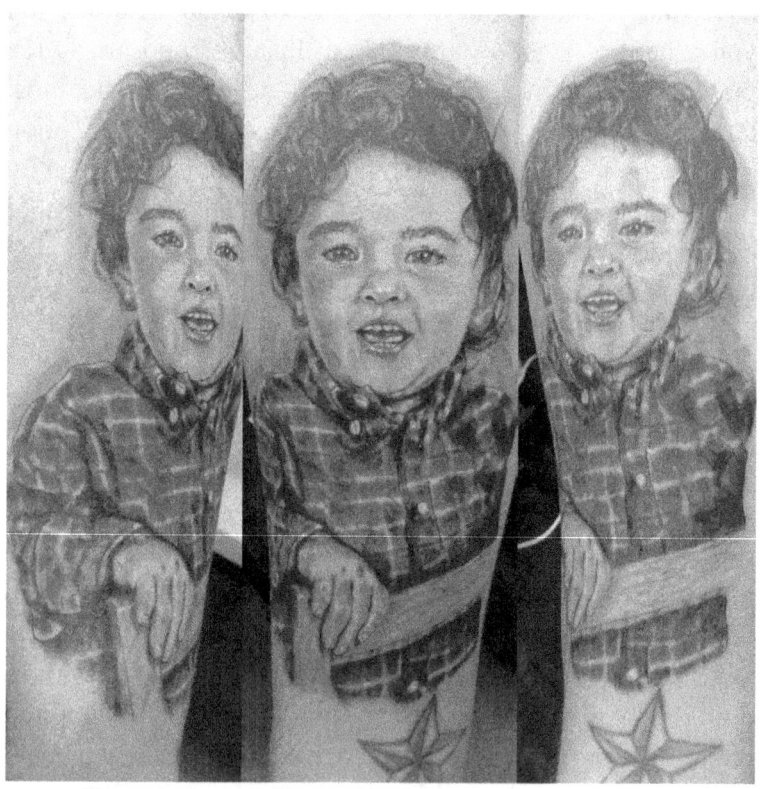

Tattoo Art by Jarris Vonzombie | Kindle book contains color photo

Chapter Seven

SPONSORSHIP

Company and Corporate Endorsement

The objective is clear, and your goal is simple. Secure sponsorship with a small or leading tattoo machine builder, a tattoo pigment company, and/ or tattoo aftercare company of your choice. There are now thousands of companies serving the tattoo industry, so sit back and think about which company you would like to represent. Whom you want to represent as an artist matters, and the suggestions I provide will help you on your journey to securing an endorsement. One thing I have learned and what you should note is that potential sponsors and companies really dislike it when an artist inquiries about sponsorship for the sake of sponsorship but doesn't use or know anything about their products or brand. There are times, however, when a company will approach an artist about switching from a currently used brand to their brand with an offer of sponsorship. This approach is typically for well-known and popular artists in the industry.

What are the Benefits of Sponsorship and the Target?

There are benefits to having a sponsor, but they may differ among companies. However, you can usually expect to get clothing, supplies, and various types of industry-related gear either for free or at cost. Having a sponsorship can also make it much easier for you as an artist to work tattoo conventions, as well as meet and network with more well-known top tattoo artists.

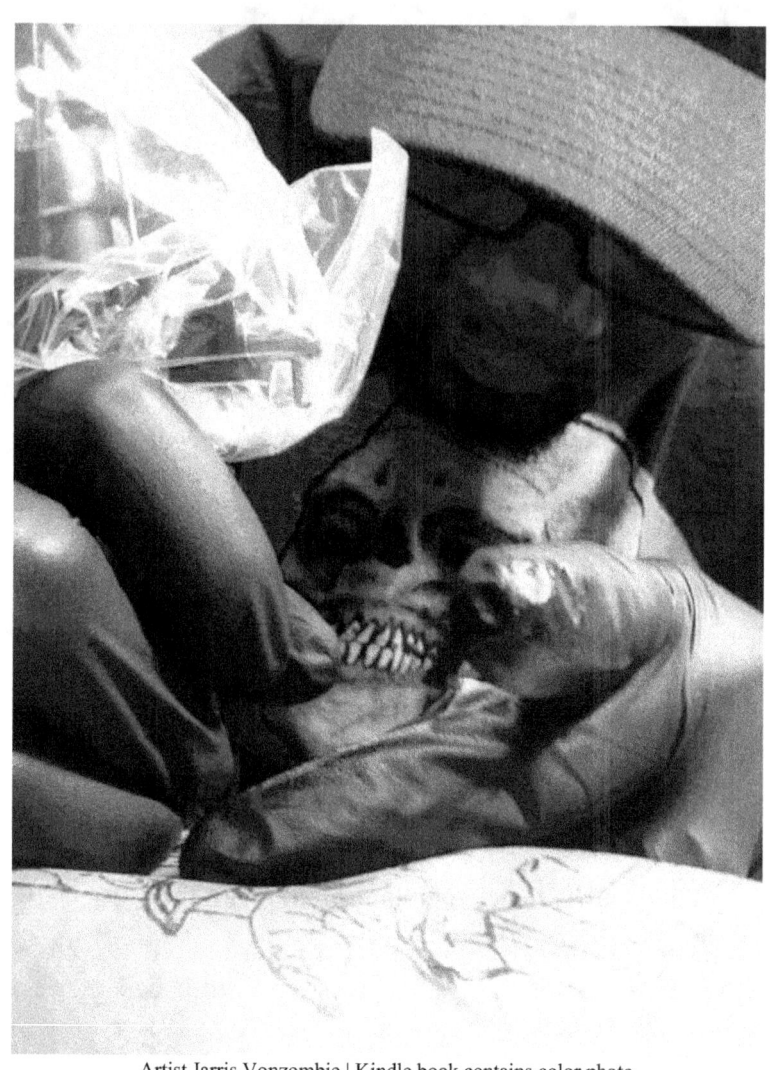

Artist Jarris Vonzombie | Kindle book contains color photo

So what's the target? Think about it. Is there a company in the tattoo field that gets you excited, a company whose ethos seems familiar to you? Maybe one of your favorite artists represents that company, or let's say that the company manufactures the equipment you prefer. That sure makes the decision as to which company you want to pursue much clearer. However, you can obtain sponsorship from more than just tattoo equipment, aftercare, and pigment manufacturing companies. Tattoo supply companies make awesome candidates. Being sponsored by a tattoo supply company means you will always have a supplier to fulfill your equipment needs. Like I previously stated, you may get your supplies for free or at an extreme discount. You may even be the first to try out new products they received from the manufacturers. That's not all; your options include companies that produce drinks, headphones, safety equipment, and of course, apparel. Focus on the big picture, think globally!

How to Contact a Potential Sponsor?

Now let's talk about contacting the potential sponsoring company. So how are you going to do this you may be asking? I have a simple answer; use the internet. Researching and finding contact information is very easy. Check the company website and social media profiles. Never be hesitant to pick up the phone and call a company. Depending on the size of the company, or let's say it's a corporation. They have persons in charge of sponsoring artists, with titles like Branding Manager, Pro-Team Leader, Team Manager, Marketing Manager, or President, Vice President, and CEO. If your local tattoo supply company carries the products of the company you are interested in, find out who they work with and see if they can get you some contact information or a business card.

You should also consider attending tattoo conventions where you can speak to their representatives directly or pick up contact information or business cards from the reps. Be organized and keep a list of everyone you have contacted, as well as note their position within the company! Make notes if a rep gives you any advice. Ask around, and network! You never know when someone you meet might be able to get you a contact that will one day help you get a sponsor.

Preparing a Sponsorship Inquiry Package

Let's put together a Sponsorship Package. This step isn't necessary, but it can help, and it never hurts to be organized with a plan. Personal websites, blogs, and social networking sites point where an artist can influence others to the point where it could be mind-blowing. The goal here is to bring everything I spoke about in previous chapters together. Your sponsorship package should include the following;

1. Your portfolio pictures and your tattoo video diaries. These can be placed on a thumb drive, or a simple link to your digital online portfolio will suffice.

2. Include the links to all of your social networking sites, links to community volunteering sites, and information about your level of involvement.

3. List all the events and conventions you have participated in or planned. Don't forget to include the links to coverage articles or online news sources about the event.

4. Include your artist features or tattoo features in any media source or publication

5. Provide a business card with all of your contact information.

6. Most importantly, include your short Artist Bio with an Artist Statement.

The Method and Techniques of Contacting Sponsors

There is always a method of getting something done, and various techniques can be used to aid the method. I have listed two techniques that are commonly used to gain the attention of company sponsors. Each technique will vary depending on the artist's personality type, as well as the scenario. Yes, personality does matter! Your personality will matter just as much, if not more than your knowledge, skill, and abilities when it comes to endearing yourself to a company while seeking an endorsement/ sponsorship deal.

Let's discuss the two techniques and associated methods;

The Sniper

Utilized when your focus is to get sponsored by a single company. In this case, before contacting this company, you need to have as much groundwork laid out as possible. Typically this a one-shot deal, so having a clear plan with a very methodical and logistical approach is recommended. Know the company structure, know about whom they already sponsor, and what they are looking for in an artist. Ensure your sponsorship package ready, but before you send them an inquiry, participate on their social media, using their hashtags with your pictures and videos, as well as commenting about how much you like their products. Share their posts with your followers, promote their company by linking to them from your social networking sites and act as a (non-sanctioned) resource when people ask about their products on forums and blogs.

You are an unofficial brand ambassador, so when another artist or client purchases and starts using their products, let the company know you pushed their product. Get well informed about who works for the company and who you need to contact to promote yourself with them. Keep in mind; the goal is to get them to notice you in a positive way, not in a way they may consider you unstable and a stalker. If it appears they are starting to perceive you in this manner, it's simple...back off and tone it down a bit.

However, when you feel ready, everything in your life is on point, your goal is in the crosshairs, and when you're as close as you can get to the company, pull the trigger. Send them a formal cover letter along with your sponsorship package. Ensure your formal letter and short bio fit the dynamics of the company. Remember to check your grammar and use spell check. Get a family member or an educated friend to proofread your letter. Give them a brief idea of what you have done, your style, your goals, and most of all, let them know what you can bring to their company. This includes how you as a tattoo artist will help promote their brand, as well as how you will be an asset to their business and sponsored team of artists.

The Shotgun

The shotgun approach is a more common technique used by semi-accomplished artists. The artists who typically have a lot of presence, somewhat well-known, or they are heavily involved in a local, national or international scene within the tattoo industry. Again, a strong sponsorship package is a good start, as is knowing what company and who you want to contact.

This technique is great for when you are looking at several different companies for sponsorship, and this is how growing artists will start their sponsorship journey. Your prepared sponsorship package should be more geared towards overall experience, style, technique, genre, and knowledge. Note all conventions you have participated in, received awards and experiences where you interfaced with the public as a representative of the tattoo industry. If applicable, add any involvement you've had with product design and testing on any level. Let them know you're an informed artist already prepared to provide services they aren't getting from any other artist. Send your sponsorship inquiry letter and package out to as many companies as you can think of, and see what comes back to you! Be patient. They may contact you and state they are not interested, or they may tell you that you need to improve your artwork. The company may not respond at all, but don't let this stop you. The big benefit of this contacting method is that if one company denies you, it's not the end of the world. Just move on and contact another company. There is only one down-side to shotgunning your sponsorship inquiry package; there is most likely less of a personal relationship established between you and the company or their staff.

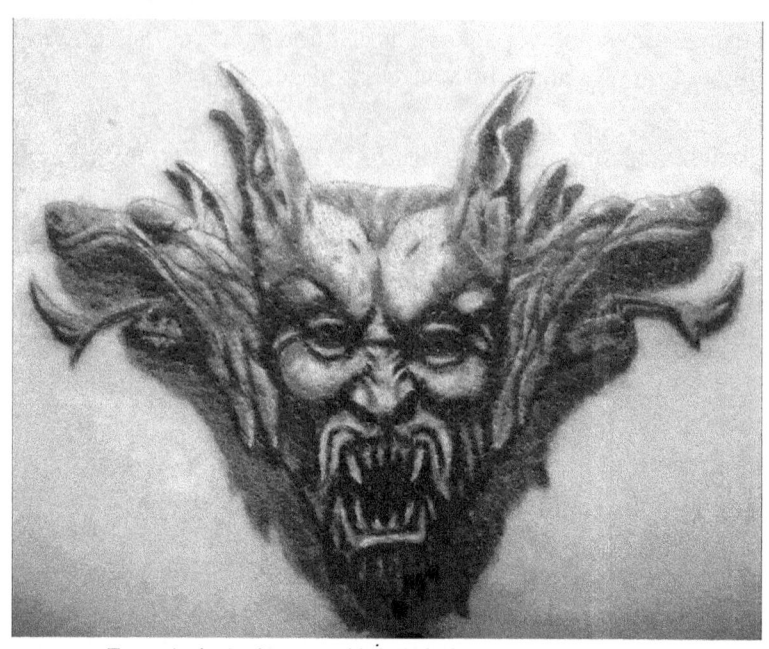

Tattoo Art by Jarris Vonzombie | Kindle book contains color photo

Now that you have had a chance to look at the techniques used to contact companies let's keep in mind that you are not just an artist but a company and a brand. So when you are looking into sponsorship, think of it as a co-branding opportunity. Meaning, you should know the history of the sponsor, look at their reviews and ask yourself, "Will your brand be properly represented with their brand?" The reputation of the company and its brands will also affect your reputation and professional brand as an artist.

Chapter Eight
RESPONSIBILITIES
Staying Sponsored!

I added this chapter because it gives a newly sponsored artist a chance to do something not many can. It is time to put a personal and professional face on the business of tattoo. There are still stereotypes and prejudices in this world, and you, as an artist, should want to break the mold and stereotype into which this art form has been cast. The tattoo was taboo; it was once considered a symbol of the lower-class and used for marking animals of husbandry. Let us not forget that many people still believe a tattoo is only for sailors, "savages," criminals, and "fast" women. Today, lawyers, doctors, politicians, and peoples from all walks of life adorn their bodies with tattoo art. It is your responsibility as a tattoo artist, whether sponsored or not, to further the art form as a profession.

When you become a sponsored artist, you are a brand ambassador, a company representative, a salesman, and a model. What you say, what you do, and most importantly, what you post online to any social media outlet will affect you and your sponsorship either positively or negatively. There is no way to quantify the value of these aspects when you are sponsored. The changing nature of advertising and the heavy use of social media by the public have been the rise and downfall of many an aspiring artist. Yes, an artist with a healthy online following is an amazing asset to a company; but negative press embarrassing a company has no value and is the quickest direct route to lose an endorsement and sponsorship, staining your personal and professional brand. Later we will talk about how to keep your sponsorship.

I have included some additional information that will be of importance now that you acquired a sponsorship. Most of what I am telling you is considered common sense. These suggestions can be useful to both sponsored and unsponsored artists. Remember, you are a business in and of itself.

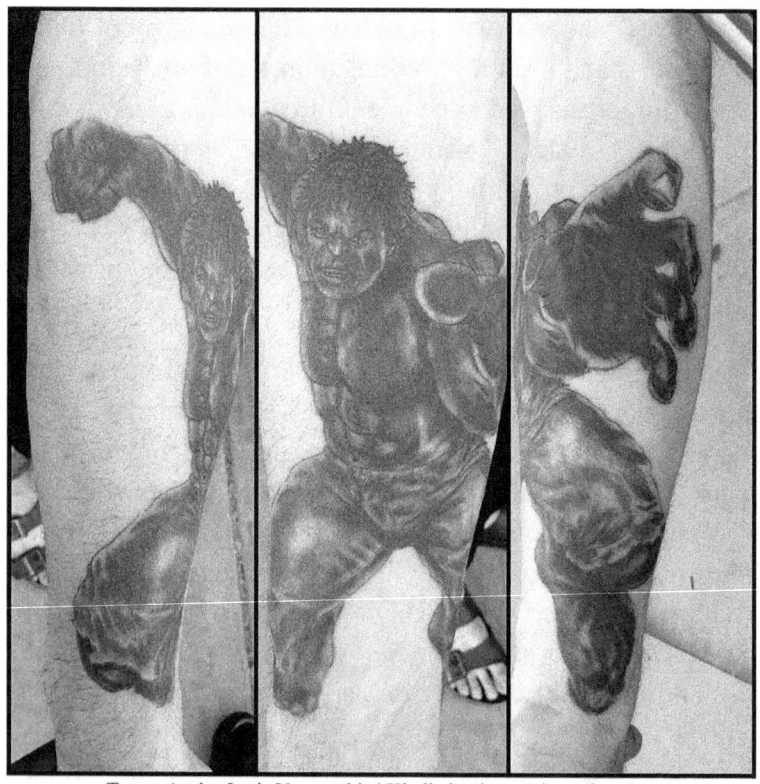

Tattoo Art by Jarris Vonzombie | Kindle book contains color photo

Spreading the Word and Helping Others Get Sponsored

Anytime you are tattooing, hanging out, or even traveling, you will run into people that are interested in you, your tattoos, your art, and possibly the company you represent. For the most part, the important thing is to be honest and to give straightforward answers to their inquiries and also give genuine recommendations. Try hard not to sound like a used car salesman! Be genuine and honest about your position and your sponsor. It helps to carry a few stickers and maybe even a catalog or two, so you can pass them out when people are interested. Always have your business cards with you, and be ready to hand them out. In this business, the best advertising is word of mouth and nothing represents that more than an artist happy to help.

Start a personal blog chronicling your activities as a sponsored artist. Fill your social networking pages with information about the sponsoring company, their products, and where their products can be purchased. Get yourself on podcasts, and when interviewed, talk a bit about your sponsor's brand and products. Give your friends and family stickers and shirts, getting them to represent the sponsor for you. Start a newsletter for the company and ad links and other current information about your company and what other sponsored artists are doing. When there is a tattoo convention or a related event, show up and represent your sponsor. Get involved in your local art scene and, when you travel, hook up with other tattoo artists.

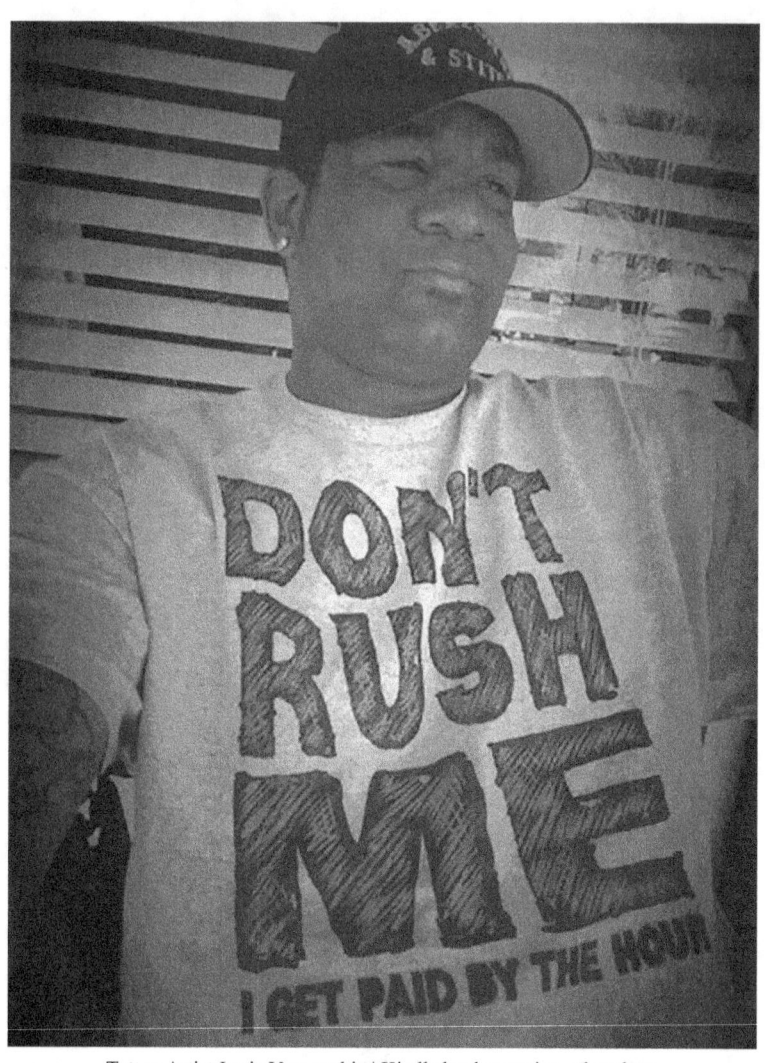

Tattoo Artist Jarris Vonzombie | Kindle book contains color photo

So should you help others get sponsored? Well, of course you should. Don't treat sponsorship like a coveted trophy; a privilege kept all to yourself because this attitude will only cause tension and distance with other artists, ultimately affecting you and the company you represent. Instead, bring them into the fold of the happening. Of course, you should know you can't get everybody sponsored, but you can make people feel involved by handing out swag. If you got a spare unused tattoo machine, give it out. If you can't get them sponsored, let them feel what benefits you do get. If you work with up and coming artists that have the skills, personality, and maturity, then groom them for sponsorship. Teach them what you have learned as a brand representative and how they too, can represent a sponsor.

One thing I stress, never, ever, allow the potential for sponsorship to be held over someone's head like a carrot on a stick to a donkey. It is disrespectful and is a disservice to the person and the company you represent. When the artist is ready, approach whoever handles sponsoring with your company and vouch for them. However, that particular artist is personally responsible for getting their sponsorship, but do what you can to make their attempt successful.

Staying Sponsored

Always try to give back more than what you have been given. Being sponsored in many ways is like having a full-time job. If you already have a sponsor, it can be fairly easy to get an additional sponsor, i.e., clothing, aftercare, pigment, etc.!

Just make sure there are no conflicting interests by checking with your current sponsor. The rest of the information I provide is just advice from what I have heard about and seen happen in the industry;

1. Don't flake on your sponsor! If you say you're going to do something, do it.

2. Don't look like a bum! Dress nice. Shower, use deodorant, put on cologne/ perfume, clean your fingernails, brush your teeth, and wear clean clothes. You never know when a photo opportunity will pop up. Represent your brand and your sponsor's brand with pride, or be ready to get potential sponsors to notice you with a sharp picture with a well-known pro tattoo artist or celebrity.

3. Don't lie or attempt to deceive the public, your clients, nor your sponsor.

4. Don't ever take your position as a brand representative for granted or try to use it for leverage.

5. Don't ever make a decision that affects the company without their approval

6. When using social media, don't post or allow for anything; photos, information, or anything that could be perceived as negative, inappropriate and/ or embarrassing to your sponsor.

7. Resolve issues with other artists or even company staff professionally. If it looks like a bad situation, always stand back, take a breath, and make sure what you do next won't be regretted because hindsight is always 20/20.

8. Be loyal to the brand and the sponsor. What I mean by this; don't be a fair-weather artist jumping from company to company within a short amount of time. Your reputation will proceed you and no one will

want to sponsor you because they will feel you lack integrity and loyalty no matter how good of an artist you think you are.

9. Most importantly, keep your technique and style tight! Just because you're a sponsored artist now doesn't mean you can slack off! Now you're being held to a higher level. Always continue to improve, learn from others and push your abilities as well as exceed expectations.

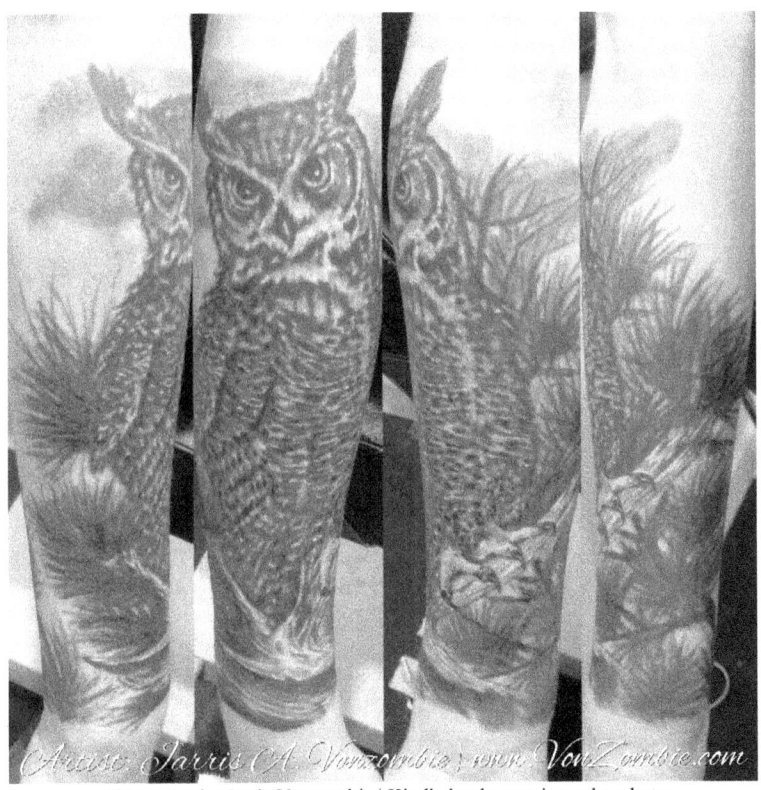

Tattoo Art by Jarris Vonzombie | Kindle book contains color photo

Keep in mind, even though you are an independent professional and entrepreneurial artist, but when you are sponsored, you will have a manager, or let's call'em a team boss. Your sponsor could be a small company of one, or a corporation employing hundreds, but there will always be someone you have to whom you have to answer. Make sure you know what they expect of you and always let them know how they can help you and how you can help them with branding, products, promotions, sales, events, etc. Always work to keep the lines of communication open with your sponsor and work to advance the knowledge people have of their brand and products.

Chapter Nine
CONCLUSION
Applying what you learned.

I hope you enjoyed reading my little book and found the information I provided insightful. I can't guarantee my methods will work for you personally, but they worked for me, and I believe my experiences to get published in magazines and get endorsed by companies within the tattoo industry are just the basics related to marketing and shameless self-promotion. You are your biggest fan and supporter. I feel that by setting goals, constantly and consistently striving to improve your knowledge, skills, and abilities, as well as staying focused and determined will ultimately lead to success, allowing you to set new goals to further your success as a professional artist.

By the way, I was able to achieve getting featured in a few magazines and gain a few endorsement deals within three years from the time I set my goals into motion in 2013. Also, keep this in mind; depending on the skill level of the artist, the strength of the artist's portfolio, the recognition the artist has received, whom they know, and how the artist carries himself in public, as well as within their social media pages will ultimately determine how long it will take you as an artist to achieve the goal of being sponsored. There are many factors, it could take one year or it could take five years, but I am sure if you spent the time to read this book in its entirety, then you will most likely be the same person who achieves their goals no matter how long it takes.

Whether you're looking to be featured and sponsored so to grow your clientele, open more opportunities, wanting to gain celebrity status, or in it just for the money. Networking is one of the keys, and being focused is a virtue. Also, keep in mind; if you feel sharp, then you will be sharp!

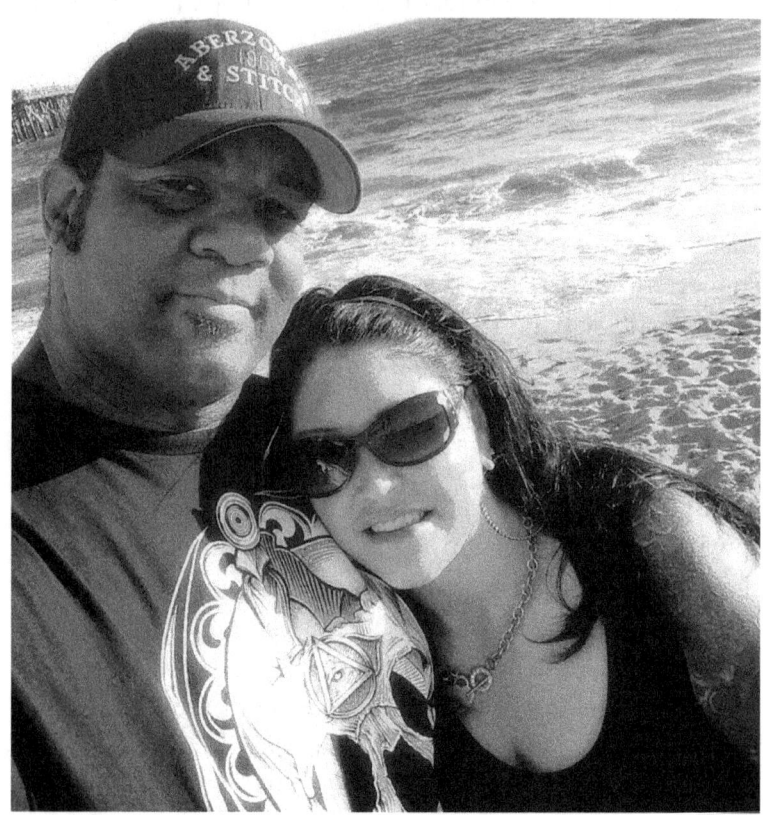

Artist Jarris Vonzombie and wife, Professional Body Piercer DeeDee Vonzombie
|Kindle book contains color photo

*My fellow artists and business professionals,
I wish you much Success in all your endeavors!*

A final helpful thought to remember;

*"Failing to plan means
You're planning to Fail!"*

Planning is one of many keys to being a successful artist and entrepreneur.

Look for **Book Two** of this series!
"Tips on How to Open a Tattoo Art Studio"

www.ingramcontent.com/pod-product-compliance
Lightning Source LLC
Chambersburg PA
CBHW070821220526
45466CB00002B/733